SUCCESS NOW– WHY WAIT!

Learning Annex® titles published by Berkley
COMPUTER KEYBOARDING IN 4 HOURS
HOW TO COOK A GOURMET MEAL IN 15 MINUTES
HOW TO TALK SPORTS TO MEN
HOW TO WIN ON THE TELEPHONE
SUCCESS NOW—WHY WAIT!

Most Berkley Books are available at special quantity discounts for bulk purchases for sales promotions, premiums, fund raising, or educational use. Special books or book excerpts can also be created to fit specific needs.

For details, write or telephone Special Sales Markets, The Berkley Publishing Group, 200 Madison Avenue, New York, New York 10016; (212) 686-9820

SUCCESS NOW— WHY WAIT!

The Learning Annex®

BERKLEY BOOKS, NEW YORK

SUCCESS NOW—WHY WAIT!

A Berkley Book/published by arrangement with
The Learning Annex®

PRINTING HISTORY
Berkley trade paperback edition/November 1984

All rights reserved.
Copyright © 1984 by The Learning Annex®

This book may not be reproduced in whole or in part,
by mimeograph or any other means, without permission.
For information address: The Berkley Publishing Group,
200 Madison Avenue, New York, New York 10016.

ISBN: 0-425-07377-7

A BERKLEY BOOK ® TM 757,375
The name "BERKLEY" and the stylized "B" with design are
trademarks belonging to Berkley Publishing Corporation.
PRINTED IN THE UNITED STATES OF AMERICA

Table of Contents

INTRODUCTION..7
SUCCESS IS FOR EVERYONE 9
WHAT IS SUCCESS—FOR YOU?.......................13
KNOWING AND BELIEVING IN YOURSELF 19
GOALS—THE KEY TO SUCCESS 31
SETTING FINANCIAL GOALS 35
CHOOSING CAREER PATHS 43
ACHIEVING YOUR GOALS 51

INTRODUCTION

Every person has unlimited potential for greater happiness, success and fulfillment. Most of us think: "I know I have ability and potential, and I want to stop wasting it, but where do I begin? How can I get what I want from my career, my personal relationships, my life?"

Success Now—Why Wait! answers these questions and many more. This book rolls out for you a complete program based on what experts refer to as the "universal principles of success." Apply the advice and exercise techniques this program contains, and you will be able to start right where you are now to find your own direction. You can start down that path and chart your progress with enthusiasm, pride and confidence. And accomplish success without lengthy personal inventories or expensive and time consuming psychological tests—without putting yourself under any unnecessary pressure.

Use this book to discover where you are headed and exactly how you are going to get there. You can learn to employ the single most important technique for you personally to create the success you want in life.

Does the *Success Now—Why Wait!* program really work? Absolutely. A short time ago, in a study of one group of Ivy League students it was found that 3 percent of them used this technique exactly, 40 percent used it generally and 57 percent didn't use it at all. A few years after graduation, the 3 percent who followed precisely the techniques contained in this book had accumulated more material wealth than the other 97 percent of their classmates combined. That's one example showing the results of this program which builds an individual into his or her most successful form and gives that person the greatest possible chance to stand out among his or her peers.

Life is a series of choices. *Success Now—Why Wait!* will help you make the best ones you possibly can.

SUCCESS IS FOR EVERYONE

Who succeeds?

The smartest individuals? The strongest? The meanest? The craftiest? The best connected? The luckiest? Everybody but me?

In truth, success is based on none of these factors—and yet on all of them. No single factor makes any individual successful. Many studies have shown that there is little correlation, for instance, between high school and college grades and later success. But most of the above characteristics can be found to some degree in people who do become successful. They exist, however, not as the causes of success, but rather as reflections of the greater elements that really do have crucial bearing on whether a person reaches his or her potential.

What is this vital underlying factor for success? You. All of you. Your mind, your personality, your strengths, your weaknesses, your whole self. And, most of all, your vision of yourself and what you want to get from life. The same studies that found that grades don't necessarily lead to success, also found that almost all successful people shared a common trait—a positive self-attitude and a firm, unshakable knowledge of what they were trying to achieve.

The strength of their personal visions drove these individuals to build themselves into the powerful, compelling personalities who attracted success like lightning rods attract lightning. Here are some of the characteristics common to successful personalities and how they grow from within:

DRIVE. A person who sees a path moves forward more quickly and with greater force than a person who sees a jungle. Once a desired goal is perceived a driven person can plan to reach it, instead of merely wandering through life. Move swiftly and decisively, and those around you will respond to your vision.

BRAINS. This is not the same as getting good grades. Successful people don't necessarily have better brainpower than other people. But once they have determined where they are going, they apply themselves so enthusiastically and indefatigably to learning everything about their chosen slice of human experience that they outstrip others and always appear much smarter than those around them. Their desire and focus vastly multiply their intelligence.

ENERGY. It springs, as the other characteristics do, from the zest for the pursuit of a recognized goal. The runner who sees the finish line speeds up. Most people have no finish line; they run over no known course. The successful person charts a course and fixes the image of the finish line as a goal. As a result, he or she has more energy and feels less strain.

RISK TAKING. Successful people take risks. Again, this derives from the fact that they can *see* the benefits their risks may bring them. If someone said: "Cross this narrow, swinging vine bridge, over an alligator-infested river," you would certainly hesitate. But, if you knew that treasure lay buried on the far shore, you would screw up your courage and plunge on. The successful person sees the far shore and takes the risk.

THE LONG VIEW. If you have no goal in mind, no plan to move ahead, life can become drudgery, a constant battle against fortune's slings and arrows. But the successful person always keeps the head up and the eye on the horizon. Bumps, bruises and setbacks are to be expected, for nothing is easy or certain in life. But if the goal is in view, if a path toward it can be seen, then optimism can prevail.

INSIGHT. This may express itself as a special creativity, a remarkable intuition, an unfailing judgment. In any form, it reflects the successful person's self-knowledge and concentration on a goal. Genius is said to be painstaking attention to detail coupled with a strong vision. That is what the successful individual achieves in the chosen field of endeavor.

INTERPERSONAL ACHIEVEMENT. Successful people can convince those around them to believe in their arguments, see their concepts, respect their judgments. This is because they understand the full picture of the situation, because they know where they want to go and how situations can help them get there. As a result, they can be more compelling than anyone who makes choices haphazardly. They also have greater empathy and understanding of the people around them because they have spent so much time and effort getting to know themselves. That wealth of self-knowledge makes them better judges of character, better managers and more fun to work with, and makes those around them allies in their quest for success.

What is the conclusion you can reach from looking at these success characteristics and their individual origins? That success does not come from the outside world; it comes from within the individual. Personal achievement is dependent on the whole personality. The traits successful people display reflect their certainty about where they want to go in life and the positive self-image this certainty brings.

To make yourself successful, begin not by examining the world around you, but by getting to know yourself.

WHAT IS SUCCESS— FOR YOU?

The first step toward success is to form a crystal clear image of what you want from life. This establishment of a goal is the heart of success because it gives new meaning and power to all the skills you possess. It is the center around which your personality and self-image grows. You cannot create a plan for success without first knowing what you want its result to be.

So, the first question to answer is *What is success?* That's a tough question. First thoughts may bring images of big cars, pools, private jets, beautiful people, bank vaults, villas and other tangible symbols of wealth, but those aren't success. Success is intensely personal. No two people have exactly the same definition of success. You could lose your way toward success at this first crucial moment if you don't try to define success for *yourself* and rely on what TV or movies or books or friends or teachers or co-workers say success should be.

At the very outset, it is important to realize that financial achievement is not success, but the *result* of success. You don't become wealthy; you *do* something so well that it allows you to become wealthy. A personal definition of success can't focus on the results; you must, instead, try to determine what it is you can *do* to achieve those results.

At the same time, keep in mind that, together, the results of success you want to see in your life and the tasks you determine to mark the best way to become successful must be related. If a big house, fancy car, private school for the kids and other expensive items rate high on your chart of what success should bring, don't pick teaching in most public and private institutions alone, for example, as an easy means to those goals.

The best plan for success is one in which the tasks you choose will provide the satisfaction and challenge you need to achieve your goals.

Now, let's get started developing your personal plan for success.

SEEKING YOUR PERSONAL IMAGE OF SUCCESS

Your sense of what success means for you, what it can bring your life, lies at the core of any plan for success. Everything that goes into the plan is based upon this individual vision. The following questions are designed to help you get started thinking about what success means to you.

1. Most of us have secret projects that we keep filed away deep in our minds. They may be past, present or future plans. They may seem utterly unrealistic. That is not important. Take a secret project from your mental closet, dust it off, and tell yourself about it here.

A secret project of mine is to write a book. I'd like to reach people through words

Don't dismiss an image for success just because it may seem implausible. Your desire to do it can make it plausible. People *do* quit corporate jobs to run charter windjammers off Tahiti—and wind up better off financially in the bargain. Don't repress your dreams. Examine them.

2. You are walking through the park. In front of you is a statue erected in your honor. At its base is a plaque. As you approach the statue, you can make out the message written on the plaque.

What does it say? _In honor of Lori Ann Filips Sheldon - She was a successful human being having it all - Love, happiness and health. She lived her life to the fullest._

The message on your statue is the way you want to be remembered. Your success image should reflect the aspirations of that testament. The way you want to be remembered is an excellent expression of what you consider to be the most important single aspect of your life.

3. Sometimes it seems we get so tied up in the daily requirements and responsibilities of life that we lose sight of the big questions and miss the opportunity to do whatever we want to whenever we want to. But, consider this: What would you do right this moment if you had

One year to live _Travel - See & do as much as I can_

One month to live _Re-Asses my faith_
Write my feelings
in a journal

One week to live _Resolve any conflicts_
and spend time with
family

One day to live _____

Can you make your life every day more like your life at its most satisfying moment? Why not? At least consider these crisis desires as important elements of your success image.

4. You just won the $10 million lottery. Congratulations! Now, write down how you would spend the money. Try to spend all of it.

Condo in NYC   Start Business
Beach house Cal   Artwork
Log house MI   Jewelry
Porsche - Red Convert.
Pay all Bills
Give money to
family.

Could you spend it all? Probably not. In fact, you probably couldn't spend most of it. Contrary to what you might think, lottery winners seldom change their lives that much. And, in truth, you probably wouldn't change yours that much either. This should reinforce the fact that money is not the heart of a success image.

5. Quickly, before you can talk yourself out of anything, jot down everything you can think of that you would like to do or be, regardless of how silly or unlikely any idea may sound. Ready, set, go.

_____

_____

_____

_____

_____

_____

_____

_____

_____

Think about this. Somewhere on that list lies the activity or career you can ride to great success. It's right there on paper in front of you. Which one? Look them over. Think about them. Don't rush. As you consider them, one will rise above the others. It may have nothing to do with your life right now. But don't discard it or ignore it. That activity may hold the key to your future.

KNOWING AND BELIEVING IN YOURSELF

You are beginning to create an image of what success means for you, but that image can't be completed in a vacuum. You must also do some thinking about who you are and who you want to become. Now take some time to get to know yourself.

LOOKING AT MYSELF

1. What I like about myself (at least 10 things):

a. The physical me_____

_____

_____

_____

_____

b. My personality_____

_____

_____

_____

_____

2. What I don't like about myself (also at least 10 things):

a. The physical me _____

_____

_____

_____

_____

b. My personality _____

_____

_____

_____

_____

HOW DO YOU SEE YOURSELF?

This is a checklist for thinking about yourself. Read each statement carefully and decide if you agree strongly, agree, are undecided, disagree or disagree strongly with it. You will agree with some statements and disagree with others. There are no right or wrong answers, and there is nothing wrong with being undecided. Just note how you really feel. Put a check in the space that reflects your true feelings. Mark one answer for each statement.

CHECKLIST

Statement	Strongly disagree	Disagree	Undecided	Agree	Strongly agree
1. I am an interesting person to other people.					
2. It takes me a long time to get used to anything new.					
3. I don't like the way I look.					
4. I have trouble controlling my feelings.					
5. I have ambition to achieve to the very best of my ability.					
6. If a friend were in trouble, I would probably drop him or her rather than get involved.					
7. I do not get really mad very often.					
8. I seem to be tired a lot.					
9. I handle most of my problems well.					
10. I am happy most of the time.					
11. I find it hard to get along with people.					
12. I don't finish most things that I start.					
13. I always try to be fair.					

14. I try to do what I think is right.			
15. I am seldom at ease and relaxed.			
16. I wish my body were shaped differently.			
17. I don't know what to do in many situations.			
18. I like to meet new people.			
19. I have lots of confidence in myself.			
20. I am a strong person.			
21. I solve problems quite easily.			
22. Criticism doesn't upset me if I feel I have tried to do my best.			
23. I always look out for myself first.			
24. I don't get jealous easily.			
25. I am poor at making things with my hands.			
26. I often act on the basis of feelings and emotions rather than reason.			
27. I am a healthy person.			
28. I give in very easily.			
29. Others will often follow my ideas.			
30. I'm pretty smart.			
31. I can make up my mind and stick to it.			
32. I am a nervous person.			

CHECKLIST (continued)

	Strongly agree	Agree	Undecided	Disagree	Strongly disagree
33. I feel guilty if people think well of me for fear they would be disappointed if they knew what I am really like.					
34. I'm a helpful person.					
35. I am unsure of myself when facing a new task.					
36. I find myself always looking for excuses.					
37. I tend to be critical of others.					
38. I drink too much alcohol.					
39. I don't take sufficient care of my body.					
40. I talk too much and don't listen enough.					
41. I often fail to assert myself.					
42. I give up too easily.					
43. I do not like being criticized.					
44. I love gossip.					
45. I rebel against authority.					

When you've completed the checklist, look over your answers. Then put a star (*) next to the five answers that make you feel worst about yourself and a plus sign (+) next to the five that make you feel best about yourself.

How did you feel when you answered the starred questions? What were you thinking? Why did they make you feel badly? What can you do about it? How did you feel when you answered the plus-marked questions? What did they make you think of? What is so positive about those qualities? Can you use these pluses to help work on the traits that bother you?

The preceding exercises should get you thinking about who you are and what you consider your strengths and weaknesses. Now, let's go a step further and try to draw some useful conclusions from what you've learned. Go over the exercises you've just completed and use the impressions you glean from them to answer the following questions.

A REALISTIC ASSESSMENT OF MYSELF

What are my five greatest strengths—in my business, life?

1. _____

2. _____

3. _____

4. _____

5. _____

What are my five greatest weaknesses—in my business life?

1. _____
2. _____
3. _____
4. _____
5. _____

What are my five greatest strengths—in my personal life?

1. _____
2. _____
3. _____
4. _____
5. _____

What are my five greatest weaknesses—in my personal life?

1. _____
2. _____
3. _____
4. _____
5. _____

Having established strengths and weaknesses, we can begin thinking about what to do with them.

HOW I WILL USE MY STRENGTHS

Think of 5 ways your personal and business strengths can combine in positive ways. What concrete plan can you create to use your strengths and make your success image real?

1._____

2._____

3._____

4._____

5._____

HOW I WILL ATTACK MY WEAKNESSES

Just as you should think about concrete plans for utilizing your strengths, you must focus on minimizing your weaknesses. Successful people do not have fewer weaknesses than others. Nor do they ignore the weaknesses they have. In fact, successful people are probably more aware of their weaknesses than others. But they are also better at dealing with them. What plans can you conceive for dealing with your greatest weaknesses?

1._____

2._____

3._____

4._____

5._____

Thinking about weaknesses can be a sobering experience, and may leave us with the impression that we just aren't good enough to get everything we want from life. Nonsense.

Life is not a fact, it is a creation. We are not facts, we are creations. We can create ourselves and we can create our lives. We can become anything we want to become badly enough and we can build any kind of life we desire deeply, strive for diligently, prepare for carefully and pursue actively.

The most important question, in terms of success, is not who you *are,* but who you *can become.* And when it comes to becoming, you create what you feel. If you feel important you become important to yourself. And that feeling radiates to others and affects the way they respond to you. If you feel proud, you will look proud, and act proud, and that pride causes others to treat you with respect, proving that you deserved to feel proud all along.

Having taken stock of your strengths and weaknesses, look at what they reflect as a mere starting point for building the person you want to be. Then, begin a program of getting high on yourself and your own potential, using techniques like these:

1. MIRROR TALKING. Look at yourself in the mirror. Talk to yourself about what you see. Tell yourself about all your best physical qualities. Make a sales presentation about yourself to yourself. Don't compare yourself with anyone else, just look at *you* and remind yourself that what you see is pretty darn good.

2. WEEKLY WEAKNESS. You can't improve yourself all at once. It is too large and encompassing a task. Improve one specific aspect of yourself at a time. Each week choose one concrete way of improving yourself. It can be physical—hair, clothes, makeup, teeth. It can be a skill—typing, computer programming, cooking. It can be behavior—talking less, listening better, being polite. As you accomplish small, highly defined tasks, you will feel better and better about yourself and improvements will become steadily easier.

3. BUILDING BLOCKS. All great accomplishments are actually nothing more than a big accumulation of small tasks. Set up a situation where the small tasks you assign yourself can be successfully completed at least once a week. Your desk will be completely clean at least once a week. You will make 100 sales calls each week. You will lose three pounds each week. Whenever you meet these specific goals, reward yourself.

4. LOOK THE WAY YOU WANT TO FEEL. If you dress like a slob, you feel like a slob. If you dress like a millionaire, you look like a millionaire. If there is a truism to the "dress for success" trend, it is that people who consciously select their clothes with success in mind actually feel more confident when those clothes are worn and do become more successful. Clothes also serve as a symbol that is very important in establishing people's first impression of you. Once they have formed a favorable first impression, they will deal with you more respectfully.

5. ASSOCIATE WITH PEOPLE WHO ARE LIKE YOU WISH TO BE. If you spend your time with lazy oafs, you will become, or at least be perceived as, a lazy oaf. If you want to become a writer, it is of enormous value to spend your time with writers. The company you keep is an important expression of your self-image. It is also a sound practical way to learn the behavior patterns, attitudes and personal outlook of people who have achieved what you want to achieve.

The first steps toward success: Establish an image of what success means for you. Examine yourself as the person you are now and begin to improve yourself toward becoming the person who can make your success image a reality.

When you have undertaken these first steps you are ready to move on to the major part of an effective success plan—setting and reaching real-world goals.

GOALS—
THE KEY TO SUCCESS

Success is based upon setting and achieving goals. If you don't have goals to reach, you will not excel. If the goals aren't realistic or well defined, your quest for success will be confused and haphazard. In short, goals are the absolute key to creating a plan that will bring you success.

What is a goal? First of all, it is not the same as your image of success. That is a broad unfocused horizon. The ultimate aim. Goals, by contrast, must be pragmatic and fully achievable—*now*. Goals must follow each other in an orderly progression leading toward the ultimate aim. Goals must be consistent. Goals must be focused.

Life has many facets, as does success. So, to keep your goals an accurate reflection of life, you need to have more than one goal at a time. If you focused solely on your career and had goals for no other aspect of life, the chaos elsewhere could easily block achievement of your stated career goal. Establish goals for yourself in five crucial areas:

1. CAREER. What will be your next job? What is the next major project that will show others what you are capable of? What will be your next profit mark or sales level? Who will you associate yourself with and who will you sever ties with now?

2. PERSONAL. Often a success plan founders because it focuses only on career and business concerns. But a happy personal life is as essential an ingredient of success as an executive job. Of course, each person's definition for happiness is different, but whatever your definition of a good personal life, it should be defined by goals. How much time will you spend socializing or spend with your family this week? What people will you befriend? What will you do this week to improve your personal relationship with one important person in your life?

3. MONEY. While money will not make success, it goes hand in hand with a career and is necessary to help create the personal life you want. You need money goals to keep up with inflation, to acquire objects or experiences you believe are an important part of your success image, and to provide a life-style that enhances your pursuit of other goals. Successful companies carefully project their financial futures and set up specific goals to gauge their progress. So do successful people.

4. PHYSICAL. You are judged in some measure by how you look. Also, you need stamina, health and vigor to accomplish tasks and meet your goals in your career and personal life. Set goals for weight control, stress management, general health and diet based on your situation, career and medical history.

5. PSYCHOLOGICAL. You need faith to take risks and emotional balance to cope with the expanded responsibilities success brings. You must have goals to build your faith in yourself. You need goals to help you achieve and strengthen your mental balance, enhance your ability to think on your feet and make the decisions that bring success.

In order to make your goals effective, write them down. There is something about the act of transcribing a thought that gives it a greater life than if we kept it in our heads. So, let's create, write down, organize, and plan a set of goals for success.

Write down your first thoughts about possible goals in each of the five crucial areas for success. Don't rush this process. It may take several days or even weeks before you decide on a first set of goals that feels just right. Keep tinkering until you can't change a thing. These are crucial choices, don't take them lightly.

WRITING OUT GOALS

Career

One-month goal_____

One-year goal_____

Three-year goal_____

Money

One-month goal_____

One-year goal_____

Three-year goal_____

Personal

One-month goal_____

One-year goal_____

Three-year goal_____

Physical

One-month goal_____

One-year goal_____

Three-year goal_____

Psychological

One-month goal_____

One-year goal_____

Three-year goal_____

Remember that each of your goals must be realistically attainable and specific. Not "to be happier," but "to remember 10 new names from my Rolodex file." The more hard-edged your goals are, the straighter you'll find your path of success.

SETTING FINANCIAL GOALS

Once you have created your first set of goals, it's time to begin planning to attain them. Because money is a particularly complicated topic, money goals require important detail work up front. The following worksheets will help you establish a realistic framework for attaining your financial goals so they can support your efforts in other areas.

HOW TO SET FINANCIAL GOALS

Start looking at your goals by examining your finances. There are three considerations when planning your finances. (1) You must provide sufficient money to afford your present life-style. (2) You must provide sufficient money to afford your (presumably improved) life-style one year hence, and (3) You must earn sufficient money to afford your "dream" extravagance—for without that Dream, your pursuit of success won't have the same vigor.

HOW TO CALCULATE OUR FINANCIAL "OVERHEAD"

How much must I spend every *month* to support my present life-style?

Rent or mortgage payments .... $_____
Household utilities .... $_____
Food .... $_____
Car Expenses:
    Payments.................................. $_____
    Gas....................................... $_____
    Garage.................................... $_____
    Repairs .... $_____
    Insurance .... $_____
Clothing .... $_____
Children's education .... $_____
Magazines, newspapers, subscriptions .... $_____
Cigarettes .... $_____
Entertainment—movies & dining out .... $_____
Insurance:
    Home...................................... $_____
    Personal .... $_____
Annual vacation—pro-rated monthly .... $_____
Other:
    What?_____ .... $_____
    What?_____ .... $_____
Savings .... $_____

TOTAL Monthly Expenses...................... $_____

MY MONTHLY BALANCE SHEET

How much do I earn after taxes every month? ..... $_____

How much do I spend each month? (see above).... $_____

Deduct how much I spend from what I earn .... $_____

Am I in the hole each month? .... Yes [   ]   No [   ]
Or am I making a profit on myself? ..... Yes [   ]   No [   ]

If I were fired today, how long would
   it take me to find another job? .... _____ months

If I were fired today, how long could
   I live on my savings? .... _____ months

MY FINANCES IN ONE YEAR—
HOW WILL THEY LOOK?

How much will I have to spend every *month* to support my improved life style in one year?

Rent or mortgage payments	$_____
Household utilities	$_____
Food	$_____
Car Expenses:	
Payments	$_____
Gas	$_____
Garage	$_____
Repairs	$_____
Insurance	$_____
Clothing	$_____
Children's education	$_____
Magazines, newspapers, subscriptions	$_____
Cigarettes	$_____
Entertainment—movies & dining out	$_____
Insurance:	
Home	$_____
Personal	$_____
Annual vacation—pro-rated monthly	$_____
Other:	
What?_____	$_____
What?_____	$_____
Savings	$_____
TOTAL Monthly Expenses	$_____

MY MONTHLY BALANCE SHEET—ONE YEAR HENCE

How much will I earn after taxes every month? .... $_____

How much will I spend each month? (see above)... $_____

Deduct how much I will spend from
what I will earn .... $_____

Will I be in the hole each month? .... Yes [   ] No [   ]
Or will I be making a profit on myself? .. Yes [   ] No [   ]

If I were fired in a year, how long would
   it take me to find another job? .... _____months

If I were fired in a year, how long could
   I live on my savings? .... _____months

FIGURING THE COST EACH MONTH FOR THE "DREAM"?

How much money will my Dream cost me? .... $_____

In how many months do I want the
     Dream? .... $_____months

How much will I have to save each month to
   afford my Dream? (After borrowings) .... $_____

MY FINANCES IN THREE YEARS—HOW WILL THEY LOOK?

How much will I have to spend every *month* to support my much improved life style in three years?

Rent or mortgage payments .... $_____
Household utilities .... $_____
Food .... $_____
Car Expenses:
    Payments.................................. $_____
    Gas....................................... $_____
    Garage.................................... $_____
    Repairs .... $_____
    Insurance .... $_____
Clothing .... $_____
Children's education .... $_____
Magazines, newspapers, subscriptions .... $_____
Cigarettes .... $_____
Entertainment—movies & dining out .... $_____
Insurance:
    Home..................................... $_____
    Personal .... $_____
Annual vacation—pro-rated monthly .... $_____
Other:
    What?_____ .... $_____
    What?_____ .... $_____
Savings .... $_____

TOTAL Monthly Expenses...................... $_____

MY ESTIMATED MONTHLY BALANCE SHEET— THREE YEARS HENCE

How much will I earn after taxes every month? .... $_____

How much will I spend each month? (see above)... $_____

Deduct how much I will spend from
what I will earn .... $_____

Will I be in the hole each month?....... Yes [   ]   No [   ]
Or will I be making a profit on myself? .. Yes [   ]   No [   ]

If I were fired, how long would
   it take me to find another job?.......... _____ months

If I were fired, how long could
   I live on my savings? .... _____ months

Will I be better or worse off in three years time:
Better [   ]   Worse [   ]   Same [   ]   Don't know [   ]

You can use these worksheets in two ways. First, they can help you lay out how you will achieve the financial goals you have set. At the same time, they can point out instantly where your goals are out of line or unrealistic. If the goals you have chosen and the worksheets don't agree, revise the goals. Goals must reflect the real world, which—after all—is where success lies.

CHOOSING CAREER PATHS

Creating career goals that fully and accurately reflect your best path toward success is a tricky business. Let's look at some of the elements that go into career success. It's valuable background for checking your own first venture into planning job progress.

There are three ways to "get the job you want" in any career. The first is to advance from the job you have toward the job you want—either in gradual stages or in one jump—within your present organization. You can move up the ladder. The second possible path to a better job is to get out of your current hutch and into a new job with a new company. And the third path toward career success is to use the experience you've garnered as a launching pad for going out on your own in your current field, or a totally different one.

These three paths are very different, but they are intricately interrelated. Most successful careers use all three paths at different times. When you are establishing career goals, consider not only the fact that you are moving, but which path you plan to move along at each decision point. This is very important because the elements for a successful career move are different for each path.

Here are worksheets for evaluating the job you have and whether it is best to move ahead or look elsewhere for opportunity.

MY SUCCESS ON THE JOB

In any job there are always "keys to success." What are the keys to success in my present job? How would I rate myself on each of them on a scale of 1 to 10?

Keys To Success   Rating

1._____ [   ]

2._____ [   ]

3._____ [   ]

4._____ [   ]

5._____ [   ]

6._____ [   ]

If I had to think about myself, where would I fit in?

          "People" Person x x x x x x x x Desk Person
   Accomplishment-Oriented x x x x x x x x Money-Oriented
       Idea/Creative Person x x x x x x x x People Manager
                    Verbal x x x x x x x x Numbers-Oriented
         Bookish/Academic x x x x x x x x Street Smart
                Gregarious x x x x x x x x Private Person
                     Sales x x x x x x x x Engineering

What are the three greatest pleasures my job has given me in the last three years?

1._____

2._____

3._____

What are three greatest annoyances my job has provided me in the past three years?

1._____

2._____

3._____

THE POTENTIAL OF MY PRESENT JOB

Many people ignore the potential of their present job. They allow their job's less exciting aspects to irritate them. They ignore their job's real potential. They ignore the potential for growth within their present organization. This is sad, since there are often more opportunities in one's own backyard than in someone else's. Here are some questions that may help you analyze the potential of your present job:

Am I generally happy in my present job? ...... Yes [ ]   No [ ]   Don't Know [ ]

Will my present job satisfy my present goals? ..... Yes [ ]   No [ ]   Don't Know [ ]

Will my present employer satisfy my present goals? .... Yes [ ]   No [ ]   Don't Know [ ]

Can I advance to a better job with my present employer? . Yes [ ]   No [ ]   Don't Know [ ]

When can I realistically look forward to that better job? .... ─────────────────────, 19___

What skills will my new job require which I do not possess today?

1. _____

2. _____

3. _____

4. _____

5. _____

What specific steps will I take to acquire these skills?

1. _____

2. _____

3. _____

4. _____

5. _____

A NEW JOB

If, when you finish these sheets you feel eager to press on, plan your goals for advancement where you are. If, on the other hand, they leave you nervous and uncertain, you might begin thinking about success that lies elsewhere. As you begin surveying for the perfect job away from your present office, remember that the best way of finding the correct job is to find:

A. The industry that excites you,

B. The company or organization that excites you,

C. The position or work that excites you,

D. The potential boss who excites you,
and then go tell him or her the twelve absolutely incontrovertible reasons why he or she needs you NOW!

This method of finding a job is more time consuming than all the conventional ways, such as sending out resumés, contacting headhunting firms, checking classified ads, etc. It is also more effective at finding a more meaningful and, often, higher paying job.

There are two keys to this method:

1. You must be willing to spend the time to do the research.

2. You must believe that all firms have open positions—assuming you can convince them of what you can do for them.

A Warning:

Resist seeking advice from friends. Stay with experts. Underachievers will accept their friends' advice. It's free. They will hear what they wanted to hear. Experts can be brutally honest. It is your career!! Treasure it.

PERSONAL RESEARCH TECHNIQUES FOR FINDING MY NEW JOB . . .

Here are some research techniques for finding a truly exciting new job. Check off those which make sense for you:

Spend two weeks of evenings and weekends in the local library reading last year's general business press.. [ ]

Speak to friends and acquaintances who seem to be genuinely having fun with their work................ [ ]

Seek appointments with business and community leaders and ask their advice on local "opportunities"... [ ]

Visit research analysts of brokerage firms to find information on "hot" new industries and companies... [ ]

Write a 100-page "White Paper" on what opportunities the 1980s holds for me..................... [ ]

Open a "consulting" firm and only take on assignments for companies I may ultimately wish to work for. [ ]

Seek freelance assignments with a local newspaper reporting on business stories of interest............... [ ]

Go out on "Information Interviews." Explain you're not looking for a job, but for information...... [ ]

Write to prospective employer companies for annual reports and product literature................... [ ]

. . . AND SOME TECHNIQUES TO GET IT

1. If you can't get in for the interview, send brief postcards, telegrams, mailgrams and letters explaining what you can do for the organization.

2. If none of your mail is delivered, and your phone calls are screened by an aggressive secretary, call or come after 5:30 p.m. Or learn your potential boss's habits and arrange to meet him.

3. Find someone you know or can arrange to know who knows your potential boss. This could be your present "mentor."

4. Offer to work without pay for one month. This is the same as a Money Back Guarantee on a product, except your employer pays nothing, other than any expenses you may incur for him.

5. Offer to join a training class without being paid.

6. Offer to work as a salesperson on commission without salary. Many firms will start you as a salesperson.

GOING OUT ON YOUR OWN

The third career path, going out on your own, encompasses so many potential situations that it is hard to present the possibilities in worksheet form. But there are some guidelines to think about if you are feeling confined and suppressed by working for someone else.

The first thing to consider is you. Are you the type of person who would make a successful entrepreneur? A psychological study of big independent money-makers stated that these movers and shakers were

—Unafraid of bigness
—Fully aware of the mission of their chosen business
—Unconfused by background details (they could latch onto the big issue in planning and thinking)
—Adept at abstract thinking
—Willing to gamble and make decisions on incomplete information
—Unafraid of success
—Filled with a deep sense of responsibility.

Think about yourself. Are you the person described here? Can you become that person? Would you want to? If you can answer yes to these questions, then you could become a successful entrepreneur.

But there is more to business success than personality. You need practical goals of a special sort to get an independent operation off the ground, such as

—You must have a strong sense of the product or service you will provide;
—You must have all the technical knowledge necessary to handle your business's problems—or at least have access to someone who does;
—You need the money, space and other necessities of operation;
—You need personal contacts with many types of people—bankers, lawyers, suppliers, customers, employees and more;
—You need lots of time;
—You must have an unshakable belief in the rightness of your enterprise;
—Your business and personality should complement each other;
—You must be able to plan and concentrate under difficult conditions;
—You must be willing to do whatever is necessary to survive, and then to succeed.

If you think being on your own is your path to success, base your goals on these requirements. You could become tomorrow's self-made mogul!

ACHIEVING YOUR GOALS

Now that you have a sense of how to begin working toward your financial and career aims, the time has come to create a personal priority for your goals. This is your extremely personal assessment of which goals mean the most for achieving the success that *you* desire.

SETTING PRIORITIES FOR GOALS

Place the goals you established earlier on this list in the order of importance they hold for you. What is their ranking right now—and why?

1._____

_____

_____

2._____

_____

_____

3. _____

_____

_____

4. _____

_____

_____

5. _____

_____

_____

Taking the goals in the order you ranked them, and using the information on finances and careers you developed in the previous sections, set up specific plans for achieving each objective. Use the following forms.

DEVELOPING A PLAN FOR ACHIEVING MY NUMBER FIVE GOAL

My #5 Goal is_____

_____

Is this goal specific? .... Yes [　] No [　]
Can I realistically achieve this goal?........ Yes [　] No [　]

Steps I will take to achieve my #5 Goal　　　　*Date done*

1._____

_____

_____

2._____

_____

_____

3._____

_____

_____

4._____

_____

_____

5._____

_____

_____

6._____

_____

_____

7._____

_____

_____

DEVELOPING A PLAN FOR ACHIEVING MY NUMBER FOUR GOAL

My #4 Goal is_____

_____

Is this goal specific? .... Yes [ ]   No [ ]
Can I realistically achieve this goal?........ Yes [ ]   No [ ]

Steps I will take to achieve my #4 Goal   *Date done*

1._____

_____

_____

2._____

_____

_____

3._____

_____

_____

4._____

_____

_____

5._____

_____

6._____

_____

_____

7._____

_____

_____

DEVELOPING A PLAN FOR ACHIEVING MY NUMBER THREE GOAL

My #3 Goal is _____
_____

Is this goal specific? . . . . Yes [ ] No [ ]
Can I realistically achieve this goal? . . . . Yes [ ] No [ ]

Steps I will take to achieve my #3 Goal   Date done

1. _____
_____
_____

2. _____
_____
_____

3. _____
_____
_____

4. _____
_____
_____

5. _____
_____
_____

6. _____
_____
_____

7. _____
_____
_____

DEVELOPING A PLAN FOR ACHIEVING MY NUMBER TWO GOAL

My #2 Goal is _____

Is this goal specific? .... Yes [ ]   No [ ]
Can I realistically achieve this goal? .... Yes [ ]   No [ ]

Steps I will take to achieve my #2 Goal   *Date done*

1. _____

2. _____

3. _____

4. _____

5. _____

6. _____

7. _____

DEVELOPING A PLAN FOR ACHIEVING MY NUMBER ONE GOAL

My #1 Goal is _____

_____

Is this goal specific? .... Yes [ ] No [ ]
Can I realistically achieve this goal? .... Yes [ ] No [ ]

Steps I will take to achieve my #1 Goal   *Date done*

1. _____

_____

_____

2. _____

_____

_____

3. _____

_____

_____

4. _____

_____

_____

5. _____

_____

_____

6. _____

_____

_____

7. _____

_____

_____

WHAT WILL BE MY BIGGEST OBSTACLES?

As I think back over the steps necessary to achieve my desired goals (steps I outlined on the previous five pages), what will be the five *hardest* things for me to do?

1. _____
_____
_____

2. _____
_____
_____

3. _____
_____
_____

4. _____
_____
_____

5. _____
_____
_____

Finally, establish a series of rewards for yourself when you achieve each goal. The rewards will focus you on the practical details of making the goal real. No goal, no reward.

WHAT WILL MY REWARDS BE IF I REACH MY GOALS?

As I reach my goals, I will reward myself. Identifying these rewards is critical because it will help give me the excitement, enthusiasm and drive necessary. It matters not how big or small, how expensive or how cheap my rewards will be. What matters is that my rewards will excite me.

What are the rewards I will give myself or I will achieve from someone else when I accomplish my five most important goals?

My Most Important Goals	*The Rewards I Will Give Myself, Or I Will Receive From Someone Else*
1.	
2.	
3.	
4.	
5.	

Creating, monitoring, revising and striving toward goals is the ongoing process behind working toward success. Meet no goal without creating another new one. Whenever a goal becomes unattainable, modify or replace it. Success requires control over the complex business of life for many months. The only way to manage this is to keep control over well-defined achievable portions of the greater undertaking.

It is like climbing a ladder. If rungs are not in place, there is no way to proceed. Each rung is crucial. Each goal is essential for success.

If you would like an interactive computer disk with concepts and exercises to achieve SUCCESS NOW, or if you want to find out more about The Learning Annex, please call the toll-free number, 1-800-US ANNEX, and ask to be put on the free mailing list.